W9-CFB-546

WHERE DID DINOSAURS GO?

Mike Unwin

Designed by Ian McNee

**Illustrated by Andrew Robinson,
Toni Goffe and Guy Smith**

Edited by Cheryl Evans

**Consultant: Dr Angela Milner
(The Natural History Museum, London)**

CONTENTS

What were dinosaurs?

Dinosaurs were animals that lived millions of years ago, before there were any people. Today there are no dinosaurs left.

Stegosaurus was a dinosaur that lived 150 million years ago.

Dinosaur means 'terrible lizard'. People called them this because their skeletons looked like giant lizards' skeletons.

Now scientists know that dinosaurs were not lizards. This book explains what they really were.

Giants

Most dinosaurs were much bigger than the lizards you can see today.

Diplodocus was one of the longest dinosaurs. It grew up to 27m (89ft) long. That's as long as a tennis court.

The Komodo Dragon is the longest lizard alive today. It grows up to 3m (10ft) long.

No more dinosaurs

65 million years ago dinosaurs became extinct. This means they disappeared forever. Nobody is sure why this happened. But experts have many ideas about it, as you will discover in this book.

A long time ago

The time before people began to write is called prehistory. It is split into three different parts called eras. This picture tells you a bit about each one.

225 million years ago.

Dinosaurs appeared here.

This arrow has colours to show the different eras.

Dinosaurs disappeared here.

Palaeozoic Era

Trilobites were small creatures that lived in the sea during the Palaeozoic Era. This was before dinosaurs.

Dinosaurs were prehistoric animals that lived on Earth for 154 million years. People have only been around for about the last three million years.

Mesozoic Era

Dinosaurs lived during the Mesozoic Era. This era can be split up into three different periods. Here you can see a dinosaur from each period.

Plateosaurus lived during the Triassic Period.

Allosaurus lived during the Jurassic Period.

Styracosaurus lived during the Cretaceous Period.

65 million years ago.

Caenozoic Era

Brontotherium was a big animal that lived during the Caenozoic Era. This was after dinosaurs.

People appeared about three million years ago.

People have not been here for long compared to dinosaurs.

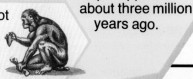

This book will tell you lots of things about dinosaurs. It will also help you to understand what might have happened to them.

3

What's left of dinosaurs

Experts have learned about dinosaurs by studying fossils. Fossils are the remains of animals that died a long time ago and have been turned into stone. They are all that is left of the dinosaurs now.

How fossils were made

When a dinosaur died, its soft parts soon rotted away. But its hard skeleton was left.

If the dinosaur was in a muddy place such as the bottom of a lake, the skeleton sank into the mud.

As more mud covered the skeleton, the bottom layers were squashed and hardened into rock.

Over time, special minerals in the rock turned the skeleton to stone. This made it into a fossil.

Dinosaur jigsaw puzzle

Scientists who study fossils are called palaeontologists. They try to fit all the fossil pieces of a dinosaur together to find out what it looked like and work out how it lived.

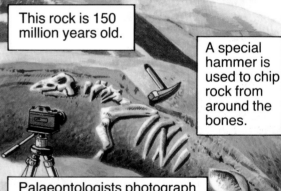

This rock is 150 million years old.

A special hammer is used to chip rock from around the bones.

Palaeontologists photograph each fossil before they remove it, so they know exactly where it was found.

Fossils are found in places that were once covered by water. Here you can see a dinosaur fossil being dug out of a cliff.

Getting it wrong

Sometimes palaeontologists make mistakes. When scientists first put *Iguanodon* together, they found one bone that did not seem to fit the rest of the skeleton. They decided that it belonged on *Iguanodon*'s nose, like a rhinoceros's horn. But when they found more fossils they realized that this bone was a spike on *Iguanodon*'s thumb.

At first they thought *Iguanodon* looked something like this.

This is the bone that muddled scientists.

Now they know *Iguanodon* looked more like this.

Experts wrap fossils in damp paper and plaster to protect them. Each one is given a number.

Fossils are packed and then taken away to be studied.

More to come

In 1965, palaeontologists in Mongolia found the huge arms of a dinosaur they called *Deinocheirus*. They are still looking for its body.

Deinocheirus's arms were longer than a man.

5

Dinosaur origins

It helps to understand why dinosaurs disappeared if you know where they came from. Most scientists think all living things gradually change. This change is called evolution.

Your environment is the area where you live. Evolution makes animals change, or evolve, to suit their environment.

Giraffes live in an environment with tall trees. They have evolved long necks to reach the leaves at the top.

From water to land

Here you can see how dinosaurs evolved over millions of years.

Over 350 million years ago, no animals lived on the land. But where pools began to dry up, some fish began to leave the water.

Eusthenopteron was a fish that used its strong fins like legs.

How to survive

Sometimes environments can change. Animals that are suited to the changes survive, but others die. A famous scientist, Charles Darwin, called this natural selection.

Not everybody believes in evolution and natural selection. Many people believe God created Earth and put animals on it as they are now.

350 million years ago, animals with legs, called amphibians, evolved. They lived on land, but they had to be close to water to lay eggs.

Dimetrodon was a reptile. Its legs stuck out from the sides of its body.

310 million years ago, animals called reptiles evolved. Their bodies were now suited to life on the land. They had dry, scaly skin to protect them from the sun.

Ichthyostega was an amphibian. Its legs carried it low over the ground.

230 million years ago, some reptiles evolved stronger and straighter legs. These were the first dinosaurs.

Natural selection at work

Peppered Moths show how a changing environment can make animals evolve.

1. Some Peppered Moths are dark and some are pale. 200 years ago there were more pale moths.

2. Pale moths were the same colour as trees, so birds caught more dark ones, which were easier to see.

3. When factories were built, smoke made the trees darker. Birds now found it easier to catch pale moths.

4. More dark moths survived and had dark babies. Dark moths soon became more common.

Shapes and sizes

Dinosaurs evolved into many different sizes. Some were quite small. Others were much bigger than any land animals alive today.

Brachiosaurus was one of the biggest dinosaurs. It could weigh more than 50 tonnes (51 tons). That's the same as nine elephants.

Brachiosaurus was as high as a three storey house.

Its back bones were light but very strong to help carry its heavy body.

Strong legs supported its weight.

Keeping warm

Animals cannot survive if they get too hot or too cold. A dinosaur's temperature changed with the heat of the Sun. In cool weather, dinosaurs got cold.

The biggest dinosaurs were so huge that it took them a very long time to cool down. So their great size helped them to keep warm.

Using a sail

Spinosaurus had a special sail on its back to keep its body at the right temperature. As the Sun moved, *Spinosaurus* changed position.

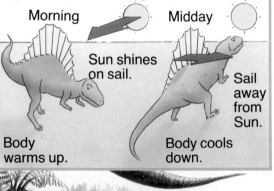

Morning

Midday

Sun shines on sail.

Sail away from Sun.

Body warms up.

Body cools down.

Different shapes

Dinosaurs evolved into different shapes for different reasons.

Ceratopians had huge heads with bony frills and sharp horns. *Triceratops* was the biggest ceratopian. It was 11m (36ft) long and weighed 5.4 tonnes (6 tons).

Triceratops had sharp horns to keep enemies away.

A bony frill protected its neck and held strong muscles for working its jaws.

Euoplocephalus was a heavy dinosaur covered in armour and spikes for protection.

Euoplocephalus used its tail as a club to defend itself.

Parasaurolophus called to others by making loud trumpeting noises through its crest.

Parasaurolophus had a bony beak for tearing off plants to eat, and a bony crest on its head.

Make a dinosaur

You could make a *Euoplocephalus* with balls of playdough, used matches and drawing pins.

Roll a big ball for the body.

Roll smaller balls for the head, legs and club.

Roll a sausage shape for the tail.

Use broken matches for the spikes.

Use drawing pins for the armour.

9

Dinosaur life

Fossil clues help experts to find out how dinosaurs lived. This also helps them to discover what changes may have made dinosaurs die out.

Clues about food

Some dinosaurs had sharp teeth and strong claws. This shows that they ate meat. *Tyrannosaurus rex* was one of the biggest meat-eaters ever. It was as heavy as an elephant and as long as a bus.

Tyrannosaurus rex had sharp teeth for cutting meat.

How you eat

People can eat many different kinds of food. You have different teeth for different jobs. Look at your mouth in a mirror and feel inside with clean fingers.

Can you feel sharp front teeth for cutting and knobbly back teeth for grinding?

Other dinosaurs had special teeth for eating plants. *Corythosaurus* was a plant-eater. It chewed on tough leaves and twigs.

Corythosaurus's jawbone shows hundreds of small teeth for grinding plants.

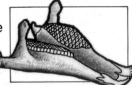

Corythosaurus →

Strong claws for tearing open its prey.

Fossil dinosaur droppings can show what dinosaurs ate.

Pine needles in dropping.

Eggs

Scientists know that some dinosaurs laid eggs, because they have found lots of fossil ones. The biggest eggs are over 30cm (1ft) across.

Baby *Protoceratops* hatched from eggs laid in the sand to keep them warm.

Staying together

Lots of fossil *Triceratops* have been found together. This shows that they probably lived in herds.

Experts think adult *Triceratops* surrounded their babies to protect them from danger.

Fossil footprints

Velociraptor was a fierce hunter. It was only two metres (6.5 ft) long, but its fossil footprints are spaced far apart. This shows how fast *Velociraptor* could run.

Velociraptor's long, stiff tail helped it to balance when it was running or jumping.

Long legs helped it to take big strides.

Fighting

Some dinosaurs that lived in herds fought each other to decide upon a leader. The thick skull bone of the male *Pachycephalosaurus* was probably used to protect it in fights.

Pachycephalosaurus fought with their heads, like goats do.

Alongside dinosaurs

While dinosaurs were living on the land, other prehistoric reptiles were living in the sea and the air. Interestingly, they disappeared at exactly the same time as dinosaurs.

Sea monsters

Huge reptiles lived in the sea. Their long, smooth bodies made them good swimmers. Their legs evolved into flippers to help them swim.

Large flippers pulled plesiosaurs through the water.

Long necks helped them to catch fish.

Ichthyosaurs grew up to 12m (38ft) long. They did not lay eggs, but gave birth to their young underwater.

Plesiosaurs grew up to 12m (38ft) long. They came onto land to lay their eggs.

Ichthyosaurs could leap like dolphins.

Sharp teeth for catching fish.

Big eyes for seeing underwater.

Ichthyosaurs had hand bones inside their flippers. This shows they were reptiles and not fish.

In the air

Pterosaurs were flying reptiles. They had wings made of skin, just like bats today. They also had very light bones to help them fly. Some were no bigger than a sparrow. Others were the size of a small aircraft.

Pteranodon's wings were six metres (20ft) across. It lived on high cliffs.

Pterodactylus was a small pterosaur. It had sharp teeth for catching insects.

Pteranodon only weighed 17kg (37lbs), about the same as a five year old child.

First bird

Archaeopteryx was one of the first birds. It had feathers and it could fly like birds today. *Archaeopteryx* lived 150 million years ago. It was about the size of a crow.

Archaeopteryx's skeleton was very similar to those of small dinosaurs such as *Compsognathus*. This shows that birds probably evolved from dinosaurs.

Archaeopteryx had feathers for flying and keeping warm.

Compsognathus was a small dinosaur.

Archaeopteryx had a skeleton like a dinosaur's.

Claws for climbing trees.

Why did they die?

Experts know when dinosaurs died out but they are still not sure why. There are different ideas about what might have happened. Now scientists know many of these ideas are wrong.

Finding out from rocks

Fossil dinosaurs are found in rocks from the Mesozoic Era. But there are none in rocks that are newer than this.

No dinosaur fossils

Newer rock lies on top of Mesozoic rock.

Dinosaur fossils

Mesozoic rock is over 65 million years old.

This shows that dinosaurs all became extinct 65 million years ago, at the end of the Mesozoic Era.

Too big?

Some scientists thought dinosaurs grew so huge that they could not support their own weight.

Now experts know that big dinosaurs had very strong skeletons.

Small dinosaurs became extinct too. So size can not explain why they all died out.

Dying of diseases?

Some scientists thought diseases made dinosaurs extinct.

Some dinosaurs did have diseases, but they evolved to survive these. Now experts know that disease on its own can never make a type of animal extinct.

Beaten by mammals?

During the Mesozoic Era, a new kind of creature called mammals evolved. (You can read more about them later.)

Some experts thought mammals ate all the dinosaurs' food.

Others thought mammals stole dinosaurs' eggs.

Now scientists are sure that mammals did not make dinosaurs extinct. Mammals only became important after dinosaurs died out.

Poisonous flowers?

The first flowering plants evolved during the Cretaceous Period. Some experts thought they had chemicals that poisoned dinosaurs.

Now scientists know that new kinds of dinosaurs evolved especially to eat the new plants.

End of the line

During the Mesozoic Era, new dinosaurs always evolved to take the place of others. But at the end of the Era, dinosaurs all died out together, and no more evolved to replace them.

Something must have happened that killed all the dinosaurs and stopped new ones from evolving. The next four pages tell you more about this.

DEAD END

Big changes

The environment changed in many different ways while dinosaurs lived on Earth. Scientists think this might explain why dinosaurs died out.

Changes in plants

Many different kinds of plants evolved during the Mesozoic Era.

These plants lived during the Triassic and Jurassic Periods.

Horsetails

Cycads

These plants lived during the Cretaceous Period.

Flowering plants

Hardwood trees

Changes in plants meant dinosaurs' food was always changing too. But these changes were so gradual that dinosaurs could evolve to keep up.

Changes in the weather

The climate is the kind of weather that any place usually has.

Earth had a warm climate for most of the Mesozoic Era.

But at the end of the Cretaceous Period it became cooler. Experts think that cold weather helped to make dinosaurs extinct.

Dinosaurs had no fur or feathers to help store their body heat. Most of them were too big to warm up again after a long, cold winter.

Changes in the Earth's surface

The Earth's surface is broken into large pieces called plates. These move around so that continents are always slowly changing positon. This is called continental drift.

As the plates move, the Earth's environment and climate change. Some experts think this made dinosaurs extinct. These maps show how the Earth has changed.

During the Triassic Period, there was júst one big continent called Pangaea. The climate was warm all around the world.

In the sea

As the land changed, so did the sea. Some experts think this killed millions of tiny sea creatures called Foraminifera, and other animals that ate them.

During the Cretaceous Period, Pangaea split up into new continents and oceans were left in between them. Earth's climate became cooler.

Foraminifera and many other sea creatures died out with dinosaurs.

Too slow

This is what the Earth looks like today. The continents are still moving, but it happens too slowly for you to tell.

Continental drift takes a very long time. On its own, it does not explain why dinosaurs and other creatures all died out so suddenly.

A sudden change

Now scientists think dinosaurs died out because something violent suddenly changed the Earth's climate. Here is what may have happened.

What broke the food web?

Many scientists think a big lump of rock from outer space, called an asteroid, struck the Earth at the end of the Mesozoic Era.

The asteroid was probably 10 to 15 km (6 to 9 miles) across.

Nothing left to eat

All living things in any environment depend upon each other for their food. This is called a food web.

Caterpillars eat leaves

Shrews eat caterpillars

Owls eat shrews

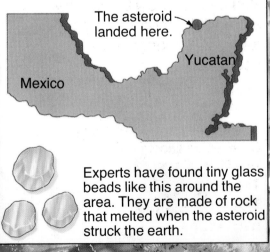

If the dinosaurs' food web broke at the end of the Mesozoic Era, they would have died out. Here you can see why.

No plants   Plant eaters died   Meat eaters died

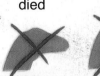

Where it landed

There are clues that an asteroid hit what is now Yucatan in Mexico.

The asteroid landed here.

Yucatan

Mexico

Experts have found tiny glass beads like this around the area. They are made of rock that melted when the asteroid struck the earth.

No sunlight

All living things close to where the asteroid struck were killed. Dust and gases filled the air all round the world. Sunlight was blocked out and the world became cold and dark.

Without sunlight, all the plants died.

When plants died, the food web broke down. This killed dinosaurs, and they soon became extinct.

How plants grow

You can see how plants need sunlight. Put some damp paper towel on a saucer and scatter cress seeds on it.

Leave the saucer in sunlight so the seeds can grow.

Cover some shoots with an egg cup.

Take the egg cup off after a week. The shoots without any sunlight will have died.

Volcanoes

65 million years ago there were also some huge volcanic eruptions in what is now India. These might have caused as much damage as an asteroid.

Some experts think dust and gases from these volcanoes might have blocked out the sunlight too.

Too hot?

When the asteroid struck, it threw up water vapour as well as dust. After the dust settled, water vapour stayed in the air. It trapped the heat of the sun, so the Earth heated up like a giant greenhouse.

Just as dinosaurs would have been killed by cold, they also would have died if it was too hot.

After dinosaurs

Not everything became extinct at the end of the Mesozoic Era. Plants grew up from seeds that had survived, and soon other animals began to fill the places left by dinosaurs.

More birds evolved to live in the air.

Small mammals lived in the trees and forests.

Some reptiles, such as crocodiles and turtles, still lived in fresh water.

About mammals

Mammals are animals that can keep their bodies warm all the time. Most mammals have fur or hair and do not lay eggs. They give birth to babies and feed them on milk.

Purgatorius lived 70 million years ago when dinosaurs were still around. It probably slept during the day, and came out at night. All later mammals evolved from animals like this.

Purgatorius was the size of a rat. It ate insects, and came out at night when dinosaurs were asleep.

Staying alive

Mammals' warm bodies helped them to survive when the climate changed and dinosaurs died out. They were also small enough to burrow holes and escape from the cold or heat.

Different kinds of mammal

The time since dinosaurs died out is called the Caenozoic Era. Many different mammals have evolved and died out during this time. Here you can see some that are now extinct.

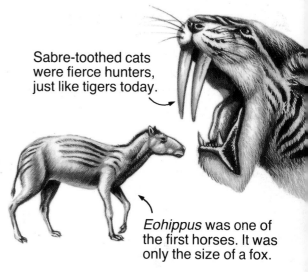

Sabre-toothed cats were fierce hunters, just like tigers today.

Paraceratherium was the largest ever land mammal. It was 8m (26ft) tall. That's six times as high as a man.

Eohippus was one of the first horses. It was only the size of a fox.

Out of the trees

People are mammals. Most experts think we evolved from creatures like apes that lived in the trees about 10 million years ago.

The first people were hunters who could walk upright on two legs. They learned how to use tools, build shelters and make fire.

Dinosaur relatives

Tuataras lived over 150 million years ago, at the same time as dinosaurs. Some still live in New Zealand today.

Tuatara

Chaffinch

Modern birds evolved from prehistoric birds like *Archaeopteryx,* and they still have very similar skeletons to dinosaurs. This shows that birds are dinosaurs' closest relatives today.

Today

Since dinosaurs died out, many other living things have become extinct. Today most extinctions are caused by the things people do.

Damage to wildlife

Wildlife means all the wild plants and animals living in the world. The main danger to wildlife comes from people damaging or changing the environment where it lives.

On the island of Madagascar people have chopped down the forests where lemurs live. Now there are very few lemurs left.

Pollution is waste left by people, such as rubbish or poisonous chemicals. Pollution in the environment harms everything that lives there.

Oil spilled in the sea kills many sea birds, such as cormorants.

Hunting

If animals are hunted too much, they can become extinct. People hunt animals for many different reasons.

Ocelots and other wild cats are hunted just for their beautiful skins. Now they are becoming very rare.

People make ocelot skins into fur coats.

Dodos were once hunted for food. They became extinct 300 years ago.

Living together

It is important to look after the environment and protect wildlife. All living things are connected to each other by food webs. If one thing disappears, many others may suffer.

For example, snakes eat rats. In parts of Africa, people killed lots of snakes. Soon there were too many rats. They began to eat people's crops, so people suffered.

Safe places

There are many ways to help wildlife. People can stop hunting animals and protect the places where they live.

Over 15 thousand elephants live in Hwange wildlife park in Africa. Here they are safe from hunters.

How to help

There are lots of things you can do to help protect your environment. Here are some ideas.

Always put your rubbish in a bin.

Never damage plants or pick wild flowers.

Try not to waste things. Re-use plastic bags and take glass bottles to a bottle bank if you can.

You could join a conservation group near your home. They organize lots of activities. You can find out about them at your nearest library.

Keep watch

Today you can only see dinosaurs in museums. But you can still see many other fascinating creatures living on Earth. It is up to everyone to stop them from disappearing as dinosaurs did.

Index

First published in 1991 Usborne Publishing Ltd, Usborne House, 83-85 Saffron Hill, London EC1N 8RT, England. Copyright © 1991 Usborne Publishing Ltd.